COUNTRY HOUSE

COUNTRY HOUSE

Janetta Hutchinson

Marks and Spencer p.l.c.
Baker Street, London, W1U 8EP
www.marksandspencer.com

Copyright © Exclusive Editions 2002

This book was created by Essential Books

A copy of the CIP data for this book is available from the British
Library upon request.

ISBN 1-84273-529-2

Printed in China

INTRODUCTION

Who at one time hasn't toyed with the idea of having a house in the country? With roses round the door, a thatched roof, the smell of baking coming from the kitchen and perhaps a cat curled up in front of an open fire. It's the stuff of which dreams are made. Ask around, however, and you'll find people's ideas on what makes a country house can differ greatly. At one extreme there's the elegant interior of a grand country mansion, all extravagant chintz drapes, polished wood and fine furniture, and at the other the more humble worker's cottage with its patchwork quilts and rag rugs.

Today's country house has distilled the decorating ideas from these two extremes and what has evolved is the look we now call country style. Once ornate tapestries used to adorn the walls of the richest country mansions. Now tapestry fabrics or embroidered crewel work fabrics can be found in a much more modest type of house. The beauty of country style, however, is that you don't need to have a house in the country to have a country-style home. Even if you live in the middle of a modern metropolis or in a suburban semi you can still easily achieve some of the delights of country style within your own home. In fact, today's country house may be found in a building never actually intended for human habitation – many people are renovating barns, farm outbuildings, cow sheds and stables and turning them into lovely homes that boast as many original features as it was possible to maintain through restoration, as well as often superb country-style interior decorations.

What makes country style so special is that it's a look with roots in the past that is just as popular today. Country style is timeless. It's neither in nor out of fashion. The style is typified by informal wooden furniture, such as dressers, rocking chairs and chests of drawers, and fabrics in a variety of patterns and colours from fancy florals to gingham and other checked designs. The trick to getting this particular interior design scheme right is to assemble it from items lovingly worn in, slightly frayed or faded, rather than those that have evidently been bought brand new. This too is the joy of

the country house. Where else would old, worn items be so cherished? In so many other interior design schemes the old has to make way for new contenders, but here a knock, chip or blemish serve only to enhance, as these imperfections add character to pieces of furniture, and to the overall feel of the home, and are therefore admired. Better still, there's really no need to co-ordinate everything to the extreme; a careful mixture of patterns and colours positively enhances the overall effect. The result is an interior that gives the impression of having been lovingly put together over time, as though each piece has been handed down through the generations.

Interestingly, texture also plays a big part in interior decoration – stone, wicker, wool, lace and brick are all found throughout the country house. They impart much of the necessary flavour that is key to achieving this style. With our current interest in all things organic, ecological and natural a second generation of materials is finding its way into the country house. Seagrass matting is becoming a popular choice – in appearance not dissimilar to the rush matting favoured years ago.

Another element of this style is that of bringing the outdoors indoors, not just in relation to the materials in which things are made, but also with regard to pattern and colour. Nothing says 'country' more than a pretty floral design. Colours used indoors relate to those found outside. Sunshine yellow, sky blue and grass green are all at home in the country house, be they painted on walls, or used in furnishing fabrics. Alternatively, earth tones such as beige, brown and terracotta work just as well, particularly when teamed with an array of interesting textures.

Yet our love of the country house isn't just about the aesthetic appeal of the interiors of these homes. It's also about how such a home can evoke feelings of nostalgia for a time when life was seemingly simpler. In reality this wasn't necessarily the case – with no electricity, running water or corner shop country life was often hard.

Nevertheless, it remains true that country style makes us imagine a time when the sun always shone, birds sang, tea was at three and everyone was happy. At the heart of a country home is the kitchen – a place that radiates warmth and to which the family gravitates. Indispensable to the country kitchen are a range oven and a large dining table around which friends and family can gather. Add to this the smell of home cooking and you have the perfect ambience of the country home.

Today's country house has far more home comforts than those of yesteryear ever had. Many of the more modest homes were simply decorated with items chosen for their function rather than their aesthetic appeal. Originally, country homes were furnished with items made by traditional methods and decorated with traditional crafts such as patchwork. You'll find traditional style is still the key in today's country home, though it's more likely that furniture and accessories will have been manufactured rather than handmade.

As the world gets smaller the list of items that now fit the country style brief is getting larger, and foreign influences have been welcomed into the fold. Shaker style, created by British emigrants who sailed to a new life in America, has returned; the simple lines of this design fit in well with the aesthetic of a country kitchen. Other elements originally found in country homes on foreign shores are also making their way to Britain. Think of Delft earthenware, Chinese rugs and Indian dhurries – a type of carpet. The result is that the country house has an ancestry that is both rich and poor, foreign and home grown, as decorative styles and furniture from diverse areas have amalgamated to create the country house we know and love.

*Bright, clean, busy or serene, the entrance sets
the scene for what lies in store inside the
country house. The hall has a charm of its own,
both serving a practical purpose and also acting
as a showcase.*

ENTRANCES

above *This uncluttered entrance hall successfully combines several materials such as timber, stone and natural fibre flooring which are all charmingly offset by a neat duck-egg blue and white colour scheme.*

Welcome to the country house

You are on the threshold of discovering the secrets of the country house. Whether you are looking for a cosy country cottage style, farmhouse or grand manor house, the importance of the look and feel of the entrance hall cannot be overestimated. It is the key to the whole atmosphere of the home.

Years ago, cottages could not boast the luxury of an entrance hall, as the front door opened into one single room which was the living area. It was only later that cottages with two rooms downstairs and two up were built, but these again would almost certainly never have had an entrance hall. Usually the doors to these homes would open directly into either the kitchen at the back of the house, or the living area at the front. On the other hand, a country manor house would feature an entrance hall possibly the size of several ordinary rooms, and in the grandest of homes it would have included a fireplace, furniture and enough art hanging on the walls to rival a gallery.

Essentially the entrance hall in today's country house serves a dual purpose. On a practical note, the hall is the gateway from the outside world into the interior of the home, which means it has a lot to cope with. An endless trail of wet feet, muddy paws and dripping umbrellas can cause wear and tear on a daily basis. Occasionally the hall is the place where shopping, heavy loads and deliveries are received. With all this activity going on it most certainly stands to reason that the decorations used here must be robust enough to withstand the elements, and yet be easy enough to clean when they suffer from their effects.

Terracotta, dusky and pale pink colour schemes work very well in the country house. A touch of spring green provides a complementary but interesting colour combination.

left *Teaming reclaimed timber floorboards with stone flooring makes for an attractive and very practical entrance hall.*

right *A country scene painted in oils in the triangular panel on the interior of the front door makes an amusing little detail and indicates things to come.*

Flooring choices

Entrance hall flooring must be tough. Traditionally, stone or tiles were used in the entrances to most homes. Patterned encaustic tiles, whose design was formed by inlaying different coloured clays which fused together when fired, or marble, the most expensive of all stone floors, was favoured in the larger, richer houses, while properties of more modest means would use simple unglazed 'quarry' tiles or flags cut from local stone. Interestingly, what was once considered the poor man's choice is now valued as a very desirable option; the cost of simple quarry tiles, terracotta or stone flooring can actually be quite high because we are no longer limited to using stone sourced from local quarries. Today it is perfectly common for a country house to boast stone flooring which has travelled from as far afield as France or Spain. So what is historically the cheaper option can actually work out to be quite expensive. Nevertheless, stone does provide a very attractive, strong and easy-to-clean floor that will last for many years, which is just the type of floor an entrance hall demands.

Wood flooring runs a close second in the range of floor coverings suitable for the entrance to a country house, as this material is also fairly easy to maintain. Traditionally, timber wasn't used for flooring in the

left *This impressive staircase has simply been painted white, and to keep noise levels down it has been partially covered with a cream carpet.*

below and opposite *Nothing says 'country' better than terracotta floors, and this well-worn example is quite a feature of this entrance hall. The faded floral curtains and the quirky child's toy all add to its appeal.*

above With a little lobby by the front door to take care of coats and shoes, the main entrance doubles as a living area. The old pine settle piled with cushions is very inviting and there's room for a table and chair too.

left and right Pine furniture makes a country home. Painted furniture looks particularly good when it's distressed – the scratches and chips all add to its appeal.

ground-level rooms, as the lack of adequate ventilation below floor level meant it became damp and rotted easily. But today this isn't an issue, so anything from reclaimed floorboards through to solid hardwood floors has a place in the country house, and this for two main reasons: first, timber has always been used indoors as flooring, albeit upstairs, and second, because wood is natural, so it fits the brief for a country-style interior design scheme. The trend today is for country interiors to incorporate 'natural' elements, whose textures and obvious links to the outdoors and countryside enhance the country feel.

Blue and yellow always make for a vibrant colour scheme. Its use is especially suited to country houses as it will bring a fresh, outdoors feel to any room. Quaint checked natural fabrics such as cotton, linen or calico can be mixed and matched to make soft furnishings.

Some country houses also boast attractive brick floors. The use of brick often starts in the porch, if there is one, progressing through to the entrance hall and possibly into the kitchen. This is an example of how flooring choices have gone full circle – several hundred years ago brick was one of the cheapest forms of flooring, often used in simple country cottages as well as in the basements and cellars of larger houses. But once again it has found favour in the country house as it can be used to create an interestingly textured floor. In some country homes rugs are placed on the hall floor. Years ago rugs were used as a form of insulation, to take the chill off a cold stone floor – but in country-style homes today a rug on the floor is usually placed there more for decorative effect than for the practical purpose of protecting the floor from dirt and excessive wear.

Colour schemes and decoration

The second function of the hallway is to serve a decorative purpose. As soon as you step inside the entrance hall your first impression of the house is formed. So it stands to reason that the decorations you choose to use here are vitally important. Our interest in interior design today means no aspect of the home is overlooked, as the chance to create, display and visually improve means no area is left untouched. Years ago only in the entrance halls to grander homes would interior decoration have been given such consideration. Certainly, if any other country house was lucky enough to have an entrance hall, it was there merely to serve a practical purpose. But these days the hallway is used to set the scene, offering a visual taster of things to come.

There are no hard and fast rules about colour schemes for the entrance hall of a country house. Any shade from white or pale pastels through to bright colours can be used. The choice depends on what type of impression you wish to create. The entrances in the homes shown here all gain something quite different from the colours in which they have been painted. Pastel shades are easier on the eye, and are a particularly good choice when you wish subtly to add interest to an area. In some of these entrance halls the clever use of pastels on the walls serves to enhance the hall's other features. For example, the powder blue walls on page 13 pick up on the muted blue tones in the flooring, and the soft pink walls on pages 16–17 resonate with the pinky hues found in the terracotta floor. Taking colour to the other extreme, bright shades always have impact. Yellow gives the hall on page 18 a sunny disposition, and is a good colour choice when natural light is limited, as is often the case in entrance halls that may only have small windows or perhaps none at all. The use of red is very dramatic. You definitely wouldn't have found this colour used in many cottages in former times; but as today's country house doesn't slavishly re-create former styles but simply takes inspiration from the past, a certain amount of artistic licence is allowed. In this house red looks good, and one of the reasons it works so well is that it echoes the richness and depth of colour of the hall's other decorations – the oriental rugs on the floor and oil paintings on the wall. Typically, decorations of this quality would have more likely been found in grander country houses, and it is in these same homes that red may have been used to decorate the walls. It was a very popular shade in Regency times, acknowledged for being a good background for pictures, and in Victorian times, with the development of chemical dyes, decorating in bright colours was all the rage. This entrance hall is by no means situated in such a grand house, but cleverly its interior decoration pays them homage.

The hall is also a place for storage – coats, boots and brollies all need a home here, and while in the past simple pegs on the wall or

opposite Rough plastered walls painted a vibrant shade of red are a fantastic choice for this small entrance hall. The colour is echoed in the rugs, bar stool (below) and floral design of the umbrella stand. A white ceiling prevents the colour scheme from appearing too oppressive.

below The use of rugs not only visually breaks up the expanse of floorboards, but protects them too.

the back of the door would have sufficed, in today's country house storage has been taken to a new level. The way in which such items are kept has become a point of interest in itself. A stand or container filled with umbrellas and walking sticks both serves a purpose and makes an attractive feature, as does a line of wellington boots by the door. In other houses such basic items as these may be hidden away in a cupboard beneath the stairs, but as these things are intrinsic to country life their presence actually goes some way to creating country style.

Furniture and accessories

Furniture can also be used in the entrance hall. Its presence is dictated more by space available than by whether or not its positioning is true to original country homes. Some form of seating is most desirable here – a chair is always preferable to sitting on the stairs when pulling boots on and off. Certainly a little table, shelf or cupboard is handy to take care of the clutter that accumulates. As long as you pick furniture designed in traditional style, there's no doubt it'll blend in perfectly. At the other extreme a very large entrance hall can almost become a family room in its own right. If there's space for a sofa or dining table the hall can double up as a more informal dining area or lounge.

As some of the entrance halls shown here demonstrate, a pine settle is made quite comfortable with the addition of a seat pad and plenty of cushions; and a large squashy sofa similarly piled high with cushions makes an inviting addition to a rather grand entrance. The idea of creating a living room in the actual entrance hall again harks back to the days when the door to most cottages really did open straight into the living area. Today, if you are lucky enough to have a hallway of a substantial size then it's a great opportunity to decorate in two distinct styles. A fairly informal decorating scheme will tend to work well in such a large entrance hall, and this leaves the actual living room or dining room available for decoration in a more formal manner.

As for which accessories to use in this area of the house, almost anything goes. From pictures, paintings, books and barometers to some more unusual

left Simple white walls provide a neutral background on which to display a variety of pictures. Wall-to-wall natural flooring adds texture, and the umbrellas make a colourful feature.

contenders such as rocking horses, clocks and chandeliers, anything that invokes a country feel can have a happy home here. As long as the pictures, be they etchings, sketchings, watercolours or oils, bear a country-related theme then they will be suitable for the walls of the country house. And what better place to put a barometer than in the entrance hall? This item, both functional and decorative (it is used for predicting the weather) is ideal for placing by the door so you can give it a quick check before heading out. Again this is an item, as is the grandfather clock, that would have been found only in grander country houses but it is now quite at home in more modest surroundings. Children's toys, such as the wooden horse on page 17, would certainly have been banished to the nursery in days gone by, but now can make an amusing piece to display in the entrance hall. And this, in essence, is what today's entrance halls are all about – an acknowledgement of styles from the past and a chance to have some fun while creating your country home.

left *A silver hanging candelabra, bearing real candles and covered in ivy, offers a very decorative form of lighting for this unique entrance hall.*

opposite *This wonderful entrance hall is quite easily achieved. The walls are roughly plastered, and the stunning spiral staircase makes a great focal point. The damask sofa covered with a rich coloured throw and some tasselled tapestry cushions is very inviting, while a large wicker basket takes care of discarded reading matter.*

As the heart of the country home, the kitchen is so much more than just a place to cook. Warm, welcoming and full of interest, it's easy to while away the hours cocooned in its splendour.

KITCHENS

A timeless look

There's no denying the irresistible appeal of a country-style kitchen. Even the most tidy-minded among us can't resist rummaging through the variety of china displayed on a Welsh dresser, or gazing in wonder at an intriguing assortment of pots, pans, jugs and tools that may hang from a beamed ceiling. In fact this Aladdin's cave of decorations is now synonymous with the country kitchen.

It is almost a prerequisite to have virtually everything you own on show in order to create a typical country kitchen. There's a homely, old-fashioned feel to these busy kitchens, which ties in very well with the nostalgic appeal of country homes. With utensils, pots and pans on show the kitchen looks ready for action – as though someone may be about to pop the kettle on for tea, or take a freshly baked cake out of the oven. In former times the kitchen was very much a working room and a hive of activity. Items most used were kept in easy reach of the cook, although there would have been far fewer items actually in use than decorate a country kitchen today. In many cottages the kitchen also doubled as the living room, and was perhaps the only downstairs room in the house.

Every item had to earn its keep, and every inch of space in these tiny houses had to be utilized. The ceiling was also made use of for hanging dried flowers and bunches of herbs. Today this is just for decoration, but in former times these items would have been brought indoors and hung to dry in the warmth of the kitchen. Baskets of vegetables and bowls of fruit are all part of the picture and along with bunches of flowers are much in evidence in the country kitchen. The presence of these natural elements adds colour and texture, creating a 'living' display. The impression they create is very earthy and organic, as though the owner of the home has just picked them fresh from the garden, or perhaps just returned

***right** Originally the range wasn't just used for cooking, it provided heat too and was often used for drying clothes. With a cat curled up on the chair and clothes hung up to dry this scene is typical of country kitchens, especially those from years ago.*

from the market. Again, this contributes to the idea that the country kitchen is the hub of the home, a place for working and also enjoying life, where all manner of activities take place.

To the untrained eye it may seem at first that the country kitchen is in disarray. However, its owner will know exactly where everything is kept. Pots and pans are usually hung near the cooker, storage jars and spices stand on the work surface or windowsill, dishes and plates kept permanently in the draining rack, glassware shown off safely on the shelves, and larger heavier items, such as mixing bowls and serving dishes, are stored below the work counter.

The joy of creating a country kitchen is often in the purchase of these items. Who can deny the pleasure of hours spent rifling through antique shops and second-hand stores in pursuit of items to display in the country kitchen? A single visit to a department store won't achieve the same result, as the key to creating an interesting country kitchen is to collect these accessories over time, and enjoy the search. From pots and pans to ceramics, glassware and utensils, baskets and storage jars, the majority of kitchen implements on show are items that should be chosen not just for their practical worth but also their attractiveness.

opposite *This kitchen's colour scheme is really appealing. The yellow colour-washed walls offset the blue and white china and fabrics perfectly, and a burst of colour from the flowers really adds impact.*

right *The kitchen is the heart of the country home, and an Aga or range cooker is essential for imparting true country flavour to the room.*

The dresser

A dresser packed full of ceramics is the cornerstone of the country kitchen. This decorative idea has been found in kitchens in Europe throughout history, although the tradition of using the dresser for display is believed to have started in The Netherlands. The use of dressers became more popular when china became cheaper to buy in the 18th century. Until then wooden platters or polished pewter plates were the norm, but as ceramics became cheaper, dinner services were displayed on the dresser. In today's country kitchen a well-stocked dresser is a must. This is not the place to practise minimalism. The more packed you can make your kitchen dresser the more attractive it seems. Mix and match is the name of the game, but in some cases a loosely co-ordinated collection of china can also look good. Those who find the heady mix of colour, pattern and shape too much may decide some semblance of order is required and limit the range of china on show to one particular dinner service, simple earthenware, or work to a colour scheme – the striking blue and white designs of Delft earthenware or Cornishware pottery for example. Whether you decide to introduce some aspect of co-ordination into this array of ceramics is up to you. Another way to make the most of the kitchen dresser is to use it to show off collections. Anything from teapots, to milk jugs or egg cups has a place here – and if you happen to collect more than one particular item you could always display one collection per shelf.

The kitchen dresser itself has changed in position, design and material throughout the ages. Depending on the fashion for household decoration, dressers have moved from hall, to dining

The palette of blues, creams and yellows suits the feel of the country house superbly. The blues echo the Delft earthenware and pottery, and the butterscotch shades are seen in the enamel of Agas and ranges.

left *Fresh produce is synonymous with the country house. A bowl full of fruit on display is a must.*

right *A modern metal pendant light has been given a country-style touch simply by being trimmed with a piece of lace.*

above This lovely room boasts all that a country kitchen should have: pretty china, tureens, jugs and jars, fresh fruit and flowers, lace trimmings and pine furniture. The old stone walls are painted white which provides a perfect background for the displays.

room to parlour or kitchen, but in the late 1800s they took up residence primarily in the kitchen, and large 18th-century farmhouses were known for their elm and oak dressers. Pine dressers were more often used in Wales, hence the term Welsh dresser, now used to describe any British dresser with cupboards in the base. Pine was also used in Ireland and Scotland more than in England for making dressers, as there was more hardwood available in England. The shelves of the dresser are called the rack, and this is positioned over a wider base, which can vary in design. Those with an open area in the base between the cupboard doors are known as 'dog kennel' dressers and it was in this open area that the soup tureen from the dinner service was displayed. A typical Yorkshire dresser features a clock in the centre of the rack, a Lancashire dresser has a cupboard in the centre of the rack and a base with drawers set on either side of a central cupboard.

Today's country kitchen is at best a visual acknowledgement of its former self. Our homes and standards of living have progressed so much that although re-creating a realistic country kitchen isn't impossible, many of us would find it hard to do without the modern appliances we're accustomed to. The most we can hope for is to take elements from the rooms of the past and incorporate them into 21st-century living. Interestingly, designers of the most progressive kitchens today are actually harking back to the styles of yesteryear and the fashion for non-fitted kitchens is emerging once again, after years of fully fitted, streamlined kitchens ruling the roost. But there is one big difference – dishwashers, washing machines, fridges and freezers are now all very much part of kitchen design. It's essential to keep as many of these modern appliances out of sight as possible – hidden away behind unit or cupboard doors, or simply curtained off beneath a work counter – if you want to replicate the true feel of a country kitchen.

The Aga

There's one item you won't find hiding behind closed doors and that's a range cooker. Nothing epitomizes the country kitchen

opposite The salmon pink walls of this delightful kitchen help create a cosy atmosphere, and with the table laid for tea the room looks very inviting.

above The hotplates of the Aga are ever ready for use and the handy rail provides a place to hang and dry off tea towels and oven gloves. Copperware is also very much at home in the country kitchen.

below Floral fabrics are a must in the country house. The delicate pattern of this material is a suitable choice as any larger designs would be lost in the folds of the Austrian blind.

below *The vibrant yellow walls and tablecloth give this dining area a sunny disposition. The use of blue in the panelling below the window and the chairs and picture frames balances the colour scheme, as it offers contrast without becoming overpowering.*

more than an old-fashioned range cooker or an Aga, developed in the 1930s. Originally cooking was done over open fires in the hearth, then when the use of the range became more common during the 19th century, these were positioned in the hearth. Originally fired by solid fuel, the cast-iron kitchen range performed a multitude of tasks. As well as providing up to four ovens of varying temperatures allowing you to cook anything from bread to porridge at the same time, and hotplates again varying in temperature, the kitchen range also heated the kitchen and provided hot water. Larger models were able to heat radiators. Today's models are somewhat easier to use and maintain, as they are powered by electricity, gas or oil. The heat a range oven gives off is welcome on winter days and in the past a clothes-horse with laundry to dry would be placed in front of it, or an airer suspended from the ceiling could be dropped down in front of the range to dry clothes. Black-leaded ranges have long been superseded by ceramic. Ceramic ranges put paid to the dirty chore of blacking the range, and these newer models also offer colour options in the kitchen. Today green, yellow, even red and blue Agas can be found in country kitchens.

Temper light bright colours such as yellow with deeper contrasting colours such as blue for a successful colour scheme. Fabrics with heavy weaves and slubs, and of course florals all add interest.

Materials and furniture

Wood and tiles are the two main surface materials of choice in a country kitchen. For the floor and work surfaces, the choice is interchangeable. Both have certain pros and cons. Wood is more comfortable underfoot, warmer and less harsh than tiles – drop something on this floor and there's a chance it may not break. Tiles,

left *When displaying china, be it on a small shelf or a dresser, prop platters and plates at the back, and put vases, mugs, jugs and bowls in the foreground. Groups united by colour always work well.*

right *Simple calico curtains with tie-tops make a lovely window dressing. Here they are hung on a narrow wooden curtain pole which complements the original wooden beam at the window.*

however, are harder, colder and, in the case of worktops, a little less easy to keep clean, as dirt can quickly collect in the grouted areas. Because of their propensity for coolness, though, tiles are a good choice, especially if you prepare a lot of pastry or handle meats. Interestingly, tile-topped tables are making an appearance in the kitchen too, as an alternative to that mainstay of the country kitchen, the traditional pine table.

Pine furniture is an essential feature of the country house, in particular the country kitchen. As a cheaper alternative to other woods, pine was originally used when pennies were tight, but now pine furniture is a staple in the country home. In the kitchen the pine dresser, a pine dining table and pine chairs are all part of the country brief. Of course you can deviate from pine and still create a country kitchen. All woods look good. But this isn't the place for highly polished pieces – the more rough and rustic the better. Pine that has mellowed with age is more suitable than the yellowy newness of modern pine, so choose second-hand items if you can for that appealing worn-in appearance. If you haven't space or budget for a pine dresser then a wooden cupboard used to form a base, with several shelves positioned above it on which to display your china, works just as well. Metal hinges and ceramic or wooden knobs on doors and drawers also add to the country flavour – and increasingly wrought iron is being brought into the fold.

The dining table is the centrepiece of the country kitchen. Before the advent of work surfaces nearly all the kitchen's activities took place on the table – cooking, cleaning, polishing and dining, even sleeping – as an unexpected guest was given the table for a bed. In former times carpenters assembled the tables in situ; nowadays you may have trouble getting large ones through the door, if indeed there is floor space for it in your kitchen. Space permitting, the kitchen table should be large enough to allow all the family to dine together. Round tables are great as they can easily accommodate extra guests when the chairs are squeezed together. The size of today's kitchen may limit your choice of table, and a gate-leg table when space is tight is a good investment. You have more scope with what type of dining chair to choose. Windsor chairs with their

left *An old-fashioned butler's sink positioned on bricks creates space so a cupboard can be built in underneath. Brass pillar taps complete the look. The edges of the work surface overlap the sink slightly for drainage without drips.*

opposite *Boasting beautiful beams, a terracotta floor, pine furniture and a range cooker, this country kitchen contains all the essential elements. The tiles on the wall and in the hearth all feature country animals.*

traditional saddle-shaped seats, high or low curved bow backs and
U-shaped arms are firm favourites in the country kitchen, since
they were designed in the early 18th century. Simpler spindle or
ladderback chairs are just as welcome. Even a long pine bench or
settle makes a suitable choice for kitchen seating. These pieces were
popular centuries ago when the settle would have been positioned
by the fire, its high back used to stop draughts. The seat can be plain
wood, or made more comfortable with the addition of a seat pad.
Rush-seated chairs also make an excellent choice – their presence
bringing a more Mediterranean country flavour into the kitchen.

The white porcelain butler's sink, which dates back to
Victorian times, has been adopted as the sink of choice in a
country home. When it was originally made it would have been
found more often in the kitchens of grand Victorian houses than
in a cottage kitchen, which may well have had a rough stone sink.
However, the butler's sink is now considered so much part of the
country home that several kitchen manufacturers have included
modern versions in their ranges in order to satisfy demand. No
longer is it necessary to search high and low for one in salvage
yards or junk shops.

Taps would have been unheard of in a true country kitchen.
Running water wasn't an option in most homes and when supplies
did improve in the mid-to-late 1800s it was mainly the grander
houses not the country cottages on the receiving end. Today of
course all homes have a water supply, so when re-creating a
country kitchen any Victorian style of tap is fine, be it wall- or
sink-mounted, or a mixer tap with an arched swan's neck design.

*Green and cream always make a great
team. Combine stronger peppermint greens
with darker clotted cream colours, or put
softer, lighter pastel shades alongside gentler
vanilla creams.*

left *The manner in which a couple of glasses
almost overflowing with flowers and a trug full
of garden produce are displayed on the table
demonstrates the casual approach one should
have towards country style.*

right *Painting the door frame green highlights
this door's attractive shape and the metal door
furniture increases its appeal.*

below *This kitchen is designed around a simple colour scheme of green and cream. The furniture is minimal – just a table, chairs and cupboard – but the impact is huge, thanks to the abundance of flowers and vegetables. It's clear to see this is a busy working kitchen.*

Look upwards in the country house and you'll most likely see wooden beams. Centuries ago most homes were constructed so that the beams and joists of the floor above were left exposed, and perhaps only the undersides of the floorboards were given plaster panelling. Of course the fashion for suspended plaster ceilings, or indeed something more ornate altogether, soon became standard in richer homes, whereas in country cottages lack of money meant beams remained very much part of the interior. And of course decorating them became par for the course. Dried flowers, hops, bunches of herbs, and baskets can all be found dangling from the beamed ceiling of country houses, with the space in between either painted white or sometimes coloured for a more decorative effect.

Colour schemes

There is no particular colour in which to paint a country kitchen. With so many accessories, furnishings and furniture providing an assortment of colours there's no real requirement to paint the room anything other than white. The kitchen will never look dull because so much else adds interest to the room. However, the use of colour can offset decorations or unite several colours, giving coherence when too many hues cause visual disorder. Yellow is an excellent choice for the walls, for several reasons. It certainly cheers up the room and if not much natural light is available the brightness of this shade helps create the illusion of light.

If you are going for such a bright colour in your kitchen you don't have to paint one matt flat coat. Paint techniques such as sponging or colourwashing result in a more mottled effect so the intensity of the colour is reduced. The unusual use of red works well as a complement to the brown shades found in this room (left) through the use of brick, wicker and wood. Oriental rugs placed on the floor echo the red in the ceiling and cleverly create balance. When choosing paints look carefully at what's on offer from paint companies. Some have a palette of 'historical shades' based on those used in houses centuries ago, and this can make all the difference in creating an authentic atmosphere.

opposite *The red walls and ceiling and blue-grey beams and door make for a very exciting, though quite unusual, colour scheme. The browns of the terracotta floor, furniture, baskets and brickwork provide contrast and balance to the scheme.*

below *Grandfather or long case clocks wouldn't have been commonplace in most country cottages. But today their presence has nostalgic appeal while their decorations can fit in nicely with country colour schemes.*

Cosiness is the key to an authentic country living room. A sumptuous sofa piled high with cushions and throws, and a real fire roaring will help your home boast true country style.

LIVING
ROOMS

The fireplace as focus

Warm, cosy, comfortable and cosseted – the living room is a place to relax, a retreat from daily pressures and a place where the family really feels at home. The fireplace is absolutely key to this feeling of comfort.

Today's country-house living room can range in style: emulating the grandeur of Georgian or Victorian drawing rooms with fine furniture, marble fireplaces and impressive window dressings, or harking back to humble cottage-style dwellings, sparse in furniture and furnishings. Today most country homes use a cross-section of these styles, put together and adapted to suit the taste and requirements of the home owner.

The focal point of the living room in a country house is the fireplace. Its original purpose in the home was to provide warmth and light on dark nights, and in the most humble one-room abodes it was the place to cook and heat water too. These days, however, its presence in a country house is more for aesthetic reasons than practical purposes. With central heating and double glazing, homes rarely suffer from the cold and the use of the fireplace, once the most important functional item in the room, has changed. A real fire first and foremost offers decoration, a focal point and a chance to re-create the look of homes from years ago. That said, nothing beats a real fire, and nothing evokes a true country image more than a dog curled up on a rug in front of the fire, or a family huddled around enjoying tea and crumpets on a cold winter's evening. There may be only a few occasions when you put it to use, on particularly cold winter days, but the joy of seeing real flames dancing in the grate justifies having a working fire in the room.

left *This beautiful fireplace is quite obviously the focal point of the room, and it is further enhanced by the balanced layout of the furniture. The glass coffee table offers respite in an otherwise richly coloured room.*

The type of fireplace can vary from a lovely, large inglenook, popular in Edwardian times when fireplaces with built-in seating were common, to the splendour of a marble fireplace, which gives the room an up-market air, or a simple little fireplace with a pine surround. In years gone by each of these styles would have had a place in a particular style of home. The more important the room, the bigger the fireplace. The material from which the surround was made also followed a hierarchy. White marble was the first choice for main rooms, but by the 1900s wooden mantels rivalled their popularity in up-market homes.

Today some cross-pollination has occurred, and styles of fireplace that aren't strictly true to country properties are being found within these homes. Yet the fact remains that a real fire is the very essence of a country-style living room and it is more important to have than not to have in this case. The more recent gas 'coal effect' fires will never be the real thing, but many models are actually very convincing as the fake coals glow just like real coals, but as they don't produce ash they require a lot less work.

The classic colour combination of red, green and cream has stood the test of time in the country house. Here creamy yellow walls are enhanced by a variety of fabrics – be they florals or stripes, all featuring russet red and bottle green shades.

below and left *Sometimes pets can provide inspiration for your choice of finishing touches. Here china dogs, a tapestry cushion and a picture on the wall (see main pic) all offer a cute little 'mini-theme' to the main design scheme.*

above *This living room combines two distinct styles – the rather grand fireplace, with brass fender and ornately decorated mantelpiece is very manor house, but the table covered with a floor-length cloth and home to an array of photographs is far more country cottage.*

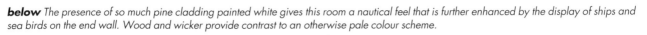

below The presence of so much pine cladding painted white gives this room a nautical feel that is further enhanced by the display of ships and sea birds on the end wall. Wood and wicker provide contrast to an otherwise pale colour scheme.

When your fire is not in use, or if you prefer not to use it at all, then it doubles up as a wonderful display area. Vases of dried flowers or even fresh flowers are typically placed in unused fireplaces, to good effect. Other accessories are perfectly at home here. Firescreens, originally used to diffuse the heat from the fire when ladies were sitting by its side, can be displayed in the hearth. Alternative ideas include piling fir cones up in the hearth as display, or displaying a collection of tall pillar candles.

Furniture and fabrics

The fireplace was the main attraction in the living room, so furniture was naturally arranged around it. A sofa in front of the fire, and maybe an armchair or two either side of the fire, are typical arrangements. Then, space permitting, other furniture such as a small table or coffee table, sideboard or cupboard can also be included. There are no hard and fast rules about what type of furniture one should select for today's country house, but you'll find most country living rooms boast simple, sturdy over-sized sofas and deep-seated armchairs, as the emphasis in this room should be very much on comfort. Overstuffed items are in order, as are classic designs that have stood the test of time, such as an old well-worn-in leather Chesterfield. The idea is not to perch primly on the edge but sink deep into the seat. Delicate, design-led furniture has no place in the country-style living room, although one or two period pieces make their way in more for their decorative appeal than the fact they are traditional country items.

below This built-in cupboard has been cleverly designed to blend in with the interior design of the room, as its sides are made of slim planks of wood painted white, while the door fronts remain quite plain.

right Several highly contrasting cushions add both comfort value to the sofa and increase the visual interest in this predominantly white room.

Apart from seating, other furniture may also be used in the living room, especially given today's requirement for extensive storage space. Again, your selection of these items may not be true to a country cottage aesthetic, but tables, cupboards and shelving should still be in keeping with a bygone era. Wood, be it pine or polished, always has a place in the country home, but other materials such as wicker, rattan or, to a certain extent, wrought iron, can also be used. The natural qualities of these materials make them suitable choices.

Continuing the theme of comfort, it goes without saying that chairs and sofas in particular should be piled high with cushions. Don't skimp on these – one meagre cushion in the corner of the sofa will not convey the idea of comfort. What you need is a whole pile – enough to make you want to dive in and snuggle up should the mood take you. Recently, throws have found a place in the country house. Their use in modest cottages was to cover up and protect the user from draughts in days of old, but today their function is to be more decorative. One or two slung over the back of the sofa lend a casual air to the room and offer a way to add colour and texture to the interior. Wool, cotton or chenille, all of which have wonderful tactile qualities, are popular fabrics for throws. Two or three of these fabrics used together are perfect for the country living room.

The size of the pattern rather than the pattern itself is really what should be taken into consideration when planning the interior design of a country living room. Use the larger, bolder patterns over the bigger expanses in the room, for example on the

opposite The most amazing thing about this room is its abundance of beams, both in the ceiling and the walls, and its prolific use of kilim rugs and cushions.

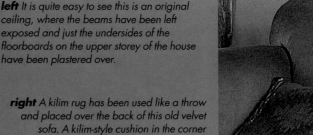

left It is quite easy to see this is an original ceiling, where the beams have been left exposed and just the undersides of the floorboards on the upper storey of the house have been plastered over.

right A kilim rug has been used like a throw and placed over the back of this old velvet sofa. A kilim-style cushion in the corner continues the Eastern-inspired theme.

sofa or at the window. Then team smaller prints together for the accessories such as tie-backs, cushions and tablecloths. Abundance is the key to successful soft furnishings. Piles of cushions, tablecloths touching the floor and perhaps overlaid with another shorter cloth. Sofas and chairs may be upholstered, but nothing suits country style better than loose covers. On a practical note it makes cleaning easier and if you're living a true country life elements of the outdoors will soon make their way into the interior of your house. Muddy paw prints and dog hairs on the sofa are just a couple of reasons why loose covers may be preferable, but they also give furniture the more unstructured look that is typical of the country house. And if these covers include frills, pleats or require ties to hold them in place, all the better. Notice how in the house shown here the window seat cushion has box pleats, and is piled high with cushions, yet the finish, far from being overdressed, looks attractive and inviting.

opposite *This living room is a perfect example of how fabrics can be mixed and matched successfully in the country house despite featuring a wide range of patterns. Here damask, chintz, checks and tapestry have all been cleverly combined.*

Don't chuck out the chintz!

Living rooms in wealthier homes were showcases for the display of the owners' taste and wealth – so if you want to go to town with interior decorating, then this is the room in which to do so. But leave all ideas about co-ordination at the door – this is not the place to create a colour scheme based on all the usual principles of

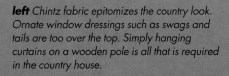

left *Chintz fabric epitomizes the country look. Ornate window dressings such as swags and tails are too over the top. Simply hanging curtains on a wooden pole is all that is required in the country house.*

right *A circle of glass is used to form a table top. It keeps the cloth in place and also prevents it getting dirty. A selection of silverware and a posy of flowers make an attractive arrangement.*

interior design. In fact, the more eclectic the mix, the better the result. As long as you bear one thing in mind, and that is not to incorporate late-20th-century designs into the room. Once you dispense with materials or colour combinations from the latter half of the 20th century such as plastic, chrome and monochromes, and select from the huge array of fabrics and materials that remain, then compiling a country-style living room becomes almost effortless.

Chintz is probably the fabric most people associate with the country look. Although it originally came from India, the popularity of this fabric in England blossomed in the first half of the 19th century, as by then it was being produced in Europe, and England had a good reputation for the quality of its chintz. Known for its patterns depicting flowers, fruit or birds, often on a light-coloured background and glazed to give it a shiny finish, this fabric was originally used mainly in mansions or manor houses. Today it has been successfully incorporated into all types of country house. For some it is associated with the out-of-date, but there's no doubt that chintz is still key to the country-cottage feel. Other materials that define the style are checks, plaids, ginghams, ticking and tartan – a clothing fabric brought indoors by the Victorians, who appreciated its heavy texture and rich colours. These fabrics can all be used alongside chintz, as the marriage of floral and geometric patterns actually adds to the country interior. Tapestry, crewel work, linen and velvet can all be used successfully in the living room. A mix of textures adds to the interior design scheme and teaming velvet with tapestry, cotton with crewel work, or damask with lace and linen all produce pleasing visual and tactile results. Better still, worn, faded fabrics will convey the country look better than the starchy newness of recently bought items. If you are buying fabric for curtains or cushions why not wash it or dry-clean it a couple of times before use to take away its feeling of newness?

Window treatments

Window dressings are an important element of any room and in the country living room curtains are a must – this is not the place

Terracotta teamed with a hint of blue make a powerful colour scheme. Terracotta is a warm shade while the cool hues of blue contrast with it well. Checks and stripes, both strong designs in their own right, also work very well together.

opposite *When a dense block of colour could be too over-powering, colourwashing walls is a good alternative – you get the colour but at a reduced strength. The leaded windows' diamond pattern works well with the checks and stripes.*

for roller or Roman blinds whose straight lines are too harsh, no matter what fabric they are made from. In fact simple curtains are almost a must – but by this we mean simple in style rather than in pattern, as anything from plaids to lively fabric designs is suitable. Unless you are dressing large windows, pelmets, swags and tails are much more manor house than simple country cottage. But don't skimp on the amount of fabric you use for making curtains; even when closed the fabric should fall in gentle folds. When hanging curtains you have two basic options – wooden or wrought-iron curtain poles. This is not the place for plastic curtain tracks. At a push you could use brass curtain poles; originally these were found in more up-market homes, but now brass has found its niche in more modest country homes – think of horse brasses here! Remember to use a pole in proportion to the window. A thick pole with fancy finials will work best at a large window and a simple metal rod is best at smaller windows, which are usually the type found in country cottages.

Floor treatments

For the floor you really want to go for something comfortable. Wood flooring is extremely popular in country-cottage style these days, but if you are pursuing true comfort then several rugs scattered on the floor are in order. Once again, poorer homes would have had rush matting or homemade rag rugs placed in front of the fire, while the floors of grander houses would be adorned with oriental rugs, pileless woven rugs such as kilims from Turkey and Indian dhurries, which are also woven carpets, imported or picked up from travels abroad. Today coir, jute and seagrass matting are becoming popular choices for the country house, especially

left *A large squashy armchair with a reading light positioned above makes an area of comfort in an otherwise quite formal living room.*

below *A colour scheme can be based around the building materials used in the room. Here the pink and cream tones found in the brickwork have inspired the colours chosen to decorate this room, and to make it more warm and welcoming.*

above The pine bench is an interesting choice for the main form of seating in the living room, and has something of the church pew about it. However, the warm tones of the wood and bricks make it appear inviting and attractive to the eye.

in the living room – despite their utilitarian appearance. Their texture and the fact that they are made from natural materials make them a good option.

Carpets would have adorned the floors of the richer homes, but wall-to-wall fitted carpets are not really what the country feel is about. If you just can't live without carpet beneath your feet, a large square carpet in the centre of the room, leaving a floorboard border around the edge, is the look you should aim for.

Favourite things

Accessories, the finishing touches in any room, can come from a variety of sources. Traditional, classic items are far more likely to say country than are contemporary, modern items fashioned from modern materials. Items once intended for a practical purpose have found a decorative use in the country home. Fire irons and bellows may no longer be required for lighting fires but they make an attractive display. Pictures with a country-related subject matter or items with a nostalgic feel, such as old tin advertising signs, can be used on the walls. Even a picture of a boat framed in driftwood evokes the necessary feel for country living. Likewise, family photographs framed in wood, silver or fabric make a wonderful collection on a coffee table. Ceramics, from simple junk shop finds to collectable china, are a must and some rather novel ideas such as an urn filled with willow branches, or miniature bay trees placed on a mantelpiece work because they continue the theme of bringing the outdoors in. At the other extreme so, too, do antlers on the wall.

The most important thing in styling the living room is to surround yourself with items and furnishings that you love, and the older the better, as what you want to achieve is a real living room where you're encouraged to sit on the furniture or handle the items on display, not regard them from a distance as if they were museum pieces.

right *Bringing the outdoors in is part of country style, and in here animal accessories are everywhere. Note the cow bells on the mantelpiece, the antlers in the hall, and the many pictures of birds, including a bird's head carved on the bellows.*

A place to relax and a place to dream. Four-poster beds, crisp cotton linens, patchwork quilts and pretty drapes are the essential elements for a peaceful and tranquil room.

BEDROOMS

Washstands and warming pans

Today's country-style bedroom still serves the same purpose as it did years ago, the difference being that now we have turned relaxation into an art form and the degree of comfort we expect from our bedroom far exceeds that required from it in the past.

A simple cottage would usually have just one bedroom built under the rafters of the roof in which the whole family slept together in one bed at night. The purely functional purpose of this room, the lack of space and the fact that for most of the year, except maybe in summer, the room would be very cold meant that no one was tempted to linger there. Even wealthier farmhouses boasted bedrooms decorated with just the bare necessities: a highly polished brass or painted iron bed with a deep horse-hair or perhaps feather mattress, and a washstand with all the accoutrements necessary for washing. The tendency was to keep clothes folded up in drawers and chests, rather than hanging them in wardrobes, the use of which became commonplace only in the 19th century. Bedroom furniture was often simpler and plainer in design than the items that featured in living rooms.

Rugs adorned the floor and the only heating in the room may have come from bringing the dying embers up from the main fire

Pink is always a popular choice for the bedroom – its appeal spans generations. Hard candy pinks can be tempered with rose or blush colours, and it always works well with cream as a contrast.

left The bedlinen with its broderie anglaise is simple and pretty, while the valance looks good being more heavily patterned.

above *Pattern is introduced into this country bedroom via the design of the wallpaper, while the soft furnishings such as the curtains and bedlinen are quite plain. The simple embroidered cotton bedding shows off these unique bedsteads to their best advantage.*

to use in the smaller fireplace, if the bedroom had one at all. However, a warming pan full of hot coals was often used to warm the bed before people retired at night.

At the other extreme, grand country houses had a whole different attitude to bedrooms. Much thought was given to their decoration and they featured beautiful curtains, cushions and bedlinen. A rather larger fireplace would be found in the bedroom of an up-market country house, the owners more able to afford to burn a fire here before bedtime than simply to rely on embers to warm the room. The size of the rooms and wealth of the family meant these bedrooms could afford to have four-poster beds. Its use today conveys luxury and romanticism but in the past four-posters were favoured far more for their practical aspect, as the heavy drapes were drawn to keep draughts out at night.

Once again, today's country-style bedrooms have drawn on influences from the past, combining the ideas from wealthy homes with the plain and simple appeal of cottage decor to make a room that offers the most appealing aspects of both.

Drapes, muslin and linen

To create a country bedroom you should begin with a bed that looks inviting – this can be achieved in several ways. If you favour more opulent styles then, space permitting, a four-poster bed is a must. Whether you choose to hang drapes from it is a personal decision, as, thanks to central heating, in most homes it's unlikely

Bringing a deeper, earthy shade of pink into the colour scheme is a good idea if you want a colour that will enhance any wood that is found within the bedroom.

left *The zig-zag pattern and use of quite bright pinks as well as pastel shades makes this bedcover appear quite modern in its design. However, it certainly looks at home in this rather grand bedroom.*

right *The use of pelmets is more country manor than country cottage, and they work best when used at a large window such as this. The scalloped edge gives the pelmet a softer finish than a straight edge would.*

below *This bedroom has an opulent look thanks to the dark wood furniture, smart pelmet and variety of rich fabrics throughout the room. Many of the furnishings have quite different heritages but work well together here as the pink colour scheme unites them.*

you'll need them for purely practical reasons. Drapes do present a wonderful opportunity to create a bed with romantic appeal. Simple white curtains can look crisp and fresh, patterned heavier fabrics will offer the room a more opulent air. An alternative idea is to make drapes from muslin. This cloth, so popular in country communities, has been given a new lease of life recently as a favourite fabric for soft furnishings. Swags of muslin suspended above a bed can create an instant curtain, taking its inspiration from the colonial mosquito net. Even if your budget doesn't stretch to a four-poster bed, simple beds made from pine, iron or brass are all perfectly acceptable and each in its own way suits the country theme. Pine was used for furniture in rooms of lesser importance and was usually found in the homes of most poor people. Today pine furniture has been adopted as the wood of choice for country-style interiors. Many country-style bedrooms boast not just a pine bed, but chests of drawers and wardrobes too. Failing that a modern divan bed can be made to look the part provided it is dressed in the correct linen and looks comfortable and inviting.

Choose your bedlinen carefully. The country bedroom isn't the place for modern printed duvet covers in garish designs, even if they are floral. Old-fashioned bedlinen may be hard work, as making a bed with sheet and blankets is far harder than simply shaking out a duvet, but if you really want your bedroom to be authentic then this is what you should aim for. In the past many cottagers grew their own flax. Flax was spun into linen and used to make bedlinen. Only since the 19th century, when cotton from America was imported into Europe, did cotton bedlinen start to appear. Now crisp cotton sheets are the mainstay of the country bedroom. The addition of lace or embroidery lends a softer, more homemade feel to the sheets and you should aim to choose this type of bedding when buying for your bed. Make sure you opt for piles of pillows or cushions on the bed, as an abundance of these really conveys the opulent look you're after. Skimping in this area will detract from the overall style of the room.

The bedroom should also appeal to your sense of smell. Finishing touches should include fresh flowers, potpourri and lavender bags. The

left *The intricate quilting makes this fantastic bedspread very appealing. Cleverly, it echoes the barley-sugar twist pedestal of the bedside table which itself is stunning in its simplicity.*

country home was often a fragrant one – not just thanks to food cooking on the range, but due to the ease with which it was possible to bring the outdoors in.

The patchwork quilt

If there's one item that has become essential to the country bedroom it must be the patchwork quilt. When you think how many hours of hard labour must have gone into making these by hand – sometimes by groups of women in a community, or by a family getting together to work on just one item – then it seems quite amazing that today you can buy lovely-looking patchwork quilts often for under £100. You could quite easily buy a new quilt and achieve the country look in an instant, but if you wish to incorporate some craft, nostalgia and history into your bedroom then buying a more costly second-hand patchwork quilt or even making your own will give you the results that no mass-produced item can ever offer. The beauty of original patchwork quilts is that they were made from scraps of material from old, worn clothes or furnishing fabrics, but also may have included fabric from a wedding dress, christening gown or other such treasured items of sentimental value.

There are no strict rules about how to decorate the actual bedroom itself. Remember that the most common time for you to see this room in all its glory is in the morning, so the look you'll

opposite Sometimes all it takes is just one or two interesting items to give a room appeal. Here the patchwork quilt and unusual bedstead do just that, and this otherwise plain bedroom is saved from verging on the ordinary.

left Patchwork quilts are actually made up in two processes. First the design is made up from pieces of fabric being 'patched' together. Then when it is finished the whole cover is 'quilted'. The stitches form a decorative pattern themselves.

right A wonderful bedstead such as this is a feature in its own right. However, a few well chosen small accessories always bring an old-fashioned feeling to a country room.

want to go for is one that is fresh, clean and pretty – one that will reflect the light and the sun coming into the room. Dark, heavy patterns or colours aren't ideal as they'll absorb too much light. Creams, pinks and yellows, or any pastel shades are well suited to the bedroom. Wallpapers with delicate designs such as sprigs of flowers work well in here, and if you're decorating an irregular-shaped room such as an attic bedroom you may even want to take the paper up on to the ceiling too. This doesn't mean that some carefully chosen bright colours or busy patterns can't be used – they can work well in a country bedroom, especially if the room is large enough for the print to be displayed to its best advantage. After all, manor houses and stately homes were known for their exquisite bedrooms with gorgeous wall coverings and curtains at the window.

Bedroom furniture

Chairs are an important item of furniture in country-style bedrooms – anything from a simple wooden seat to a wicker chair or even a soft upholstered armchair. Again, the choice depends on the space available. Just be sure to make them appear inviting through the addition of a cushion or seat pad. Other seating ideas include window seats, ottomans or a blanket box with a soft seat

left The only bright colours found in this lovely bedroom come from this delightful vase of fresh flowers. Change the flowers, and you change the colour scheme!

right Wood and white make up the colour scheme in here, and very successful it is too. The best way to show the bed off is to make sure nothing competes with it, and by choosing simple white furnishings nothing does.

above *Using a mini-print wallpaper and the same pattern for the curtain fabric unifies the colour scheme and makes the most of the space in a small bedroom, where the use of large patterns or bold designs can be overpowering.*

pad placed on its lid, usually stood at the end of the bed. For something more dramatic choose a chaise-longue. They may not have been found in the traditional country house, but having found favour in Regency times they are now considered rather decadent, as the idea of relaxing during the daytime isn't in vogue. Washstands make a delightful addition. Though no longer required for their original purpose they serve as a charming display area and can look extremely attractive with ceramics, flowers or photographs arranged on their top. A small writing desk or bureau may well have been found, particularly in guest bedrooms of grand country houses, and if there's room for one in yours it's also a lovely item to stand in front of the window – it may even inspire you to write occasionally.

Wickerwork was popular in Victorian times, and this type of furniture is particularly suited to the bedroom, as the open weave designs of rattan, cane and wicker give it a softer, lighter appearance than wooden furniture. The result is that furniture made from these materials works well in any size of bedroom, where the need for heavy, robust items isn't as important as in other rooms of the house. These natural materials also add to the country image, as they are reminiscent of a time when craftsmen would have worked items from these materials for use in their own and other local homes.

Burnt orange, beige and wheat make for a more demure colour scheme. When you're decorating small rooms neutrals and naturals are always a good choice, as paler colours make the room seem larger.

left *These curtains are one of the simplest styles you can make, as the tops are devoid of any fussy details. Hung on a wooden curtain pole they are perfect for a country-style bedroom.*

right *White china with simple floral motifs makes an attractive display on an old washstand situated in the corner of this little bedroom.*

Bedroom lighting

Years ago candles, and later paraffin or oil lamps, would have been the only form of lighting in bedrooms or often the whole house, and today these can be included, though their presence often lends a more romantic than practical element to the design scheme. Central overhead lighting is often too harsh, particularly at night, and not in keeping with true country style. Electricity started to be used for lighting in the early 1900s, but it would be much later before most country cottages enjoyed its convenience. Lamps are more suitable for bedroom lighting. Bases made from wood, brass or ceramics coupled with classic coolie shades made from fabrics such as chintz, silk, hessian or even handmade papers look best. Avoid lamps in materials and colours

left *Pretty mini-print fabrics have been used to decorate this bedroom. Although the patterns differ between the curtains, tablecloth and quilt they work well together as the colours and dimensions unite them.*

above *Crisp white bedlinen makes this bed look most inviting, and it complements the dark wood very well. The small but attractive window doesn't require curtains as it makes quite a feature left plain. The tiny child's chair also adds interest to this bedroom.*

left *The checked curtains are partially tucked away behind the high head-board of this bed. Originally drawn to keep the cold out at night, their use is more decorative now as most country houses boast central heating.*

that will look too modern – such as primary colours, plastics, chrome and modern metals such as aluminium.

A child's bedroom

If children were lucky enough to have their own bedrooms then these would have been quite functional rooms boasting a bed, a bedside table, chest of drawers, perhaps a small chair and little else. Today, creating a country-style bedroom for children is a pure delight. It's a chance to combine all the sweetest elements of country style together – pastel colours on the wall, delicate floral motifs or tiny checks and stripes for fabrics and wallcoverings, natural flooring that'll stand up to the wear and tear only children are capable of giving, and simple wooden furniture, perhaps painted or decorated with stencils or folk-art inspired motifs. Original nursery furniture is quite hard to come by but worth searching for. A straw basket, crib or tiny nursery chairs all make charming additions to these rooms – even when the occupants have long since outgrown them!

left *Teddy bears always have a place in a child's bedroom. Those made of patchwork, or a little battered or worn are particularly suitable for the country house.*

right *Stone walls painted lavender and teamed with balloon-patterned wallpaper in mint green make a stunning combination for a child's bedroom. White bedlinen is a must for children's rooms too.*

There's a lot of decorating fun to be had in here, as the source of ideas for this room need never run dry. From Victorian style to seaside simplicity you'll find these country bathrooms offer plenty of novel ideas.

BATHROOMS

above Panelled walls and an attractive dado rail teamed with a taupe sea-shell patterned wallpaper – a design reflected in the choice of towels – make for a stylish and practical bathroom with a slightly seaside feel.

Bathing Victorian-style

A place to wash, clean, maybe even lie back and dream. As a personal retreat from a busy, tough and often dirty outdoor life the country-style bathroom provides a much-needed element of escapism.

The bathroom is actually a room that wouldn't have existed at all in many country homes until the 20th century, so the style in which we decorate it has evolved from Victorian and Edwardian ideas, as this was the time when bathrooms started to become more commonplace in the home. It is possible that some of the very richest country homes may have had an indoor bathroom. The decor, however, would have been inspired by styles of the time. Therefore it could be said that the country bathroom is in some ways a contradiction in terms, as the look we refer to as 'country bathroom' was rarely found in country homes at all until relatively recently.

It was only during the 20th century that the bathroom became an indoor feature. Until then, whether you were rich or poor your toilet remained outside in the 'outhouse', which was usually situated at the end of the garden. To save a trip down the garden path at night most people kept a chamber pot under the bed, and washing was done indoors using a jug and bowl at a washstand. Baths were not taken with the regularity they are today – the old joke 'if you're taking a bath it must be your birthday' wasn't far from the truth. And when baths were taken the whole bathing process was usually carried out in a portable hip bath indoors, in front of a burning fire, upstairs in the bedroom for the rich, in the kitchen, wash-house or scullery for the poor.

This method of bathing was incredibly time-consuming, as the water needed to fill the bath had to be heated first over the kitchen fire, or in later days over the range, and the bath would then have to be filled, and of course emptied, by hand – an arduous task, as only the rich could afford the luxury of maids or servants to do this job for them.

above *An attractive shelf is made by placing a plank of wood on two wrought-iron shelf supports.*

below *A wrought-iron chair like this with a rattan seat is more commonly found outdoors or in a conservatory, but it is also perfectly at home in the bathroom.*

Of course, most old country homes weren't designed or built with bathrooms in mind, so when in Victorian times with the advent of indoor plumbing and sewerage systems the concept of the bathroom was introduced, it had to be sited in a spare bedroom, or dressing room. The Victorians would decorate it just like any other room in the house. Not surprisingly, wallpaper and floor coverings did not fare too well in damp and steamy conditions. The actual toiletries were hidden away in wooden encasements that had the appearance of an ordinary piece of furniture, such was the prudery of the Victorians. Country-style bathrooms are now decorated as thoughtfully as any other room in the house, but without the peculiarity of hiding essential items, and with more of an eye to practical concerns.

Since bathrooms were originally sited in an existing room of the house, they were often larger than the tiny rooms we are used to today. These rooms would boast a variety of features, such as a fireplace or window overlooking a good view, again in complete contrast to the modern purpose-built little rooms, which may not contain a window at all. As many country bathrooms are situated in what would have once been a bedroom, or perhaps in the converted loft space of a barn or stable, architectural elements such as sloping ceilings and exposed beams may well remain as features.

Modern, streamlined fitted units are not for the country-style bathroom. Just as with the country kitchen, a non-fitted bathroom, as much as is possible, is far more in keeping with country style.

left *The pelmet over the shelves displaying sea-shells is itself decorated with shells, a motif that is echoed in the attractive stencil round the mirror.*

right *This tiny bathroom looks lovely painted pink. The Lloyd Loom chair makes a delightful addition, contrasting well and adding some comfort.*

above A cream colour scheme and traditional fittings create a country-style bathroom. Colour is added via the accessories and comfort comes from the grand Windsor chair.

The cast-iron bath

The ideal type of bath to have in your country bathroom is a Victorian rolltop, cast-iron bath. Originally these were encased in wooden frames. Should you choose to do this, a rich mahogany bath panel is perfect for conveying the look of Victorian splendour. However, the trend for raising the bath on ornamental ball and claw feet is a look that is becoming popular again today. The exposed underside of the bath can then be painted or decorated to suit the colour scheme of the room, or as a decorative alternative a paint effect finish such as rag rolling, or a simple stencil design can look fantastic.

Space permitting, the best way to position a rolltop, cast-iron bath is to show it off in all its splendour in the middle of the bathroom or beneath a window where bathers can enjoy the scenery as they wash. As the fashion for rolltop baths is emerging once again there are many reproduction models available, so there isn't such a need to scour architectural salvage yards to find one. Failing this, an ordinary cast-iron or enamel bath is a must to evoke the feeling of a bygone age.

Adapting the modern bath

If your bathroom does feature a modern acrylic bath then all is not lost. Generally speaking, modern coloured acrylic suites are a no-no for country-style bathrooms, but if you happen to have inherited one disguise is the best remedy. Simply panelling the bath, swapping the plastic toilet seat for one made of pine and

left *Privacy is essential in the bathroom but it's a pity to replace pretty windows with patterned glass. Blinds such as these with a lively floral design are therefore a must.*

right *A simple 'skirt' made from cotton secured around the wash basin hides all the pipe work beneath, and makes a pretty addition to the room.*

below *Dark wood looks very smart and quite masculine in the bathroom, but decorative details such as the cherub designs in the corner and plenty of plants prevent the room from looking too severe.*

fixing a fabric skirt around the basin to hide the pedestal on which it rests can make all the difference. By clever colour scheming an avocado green or canary yellow suite can actually be made to work in a country bathroom, as in essence these are country colours, even though suites such as these wouldn't originally have been found in country houses. If you're blessed with a suite in a stronger shade such as purple it might be better to give it an up-market Victoriana-inspired makeover with plenty of dark wood panelling, and a deep rich colour scheme – more country manor than country house.

Fixtures and fittings

Again, it was only at the turn of the 20th century that ceramic washbasins mounted on brackets became more commonplace in the bathroom. Until then washing was done using water held in jugs and bowls at a washstand in the bedroom. The washstand was usually made of wood and perhaps, but not always, had a marble top. To convey a country feel it is perfectly possible to have a modern working washbasin plumbed into into an old washstand, which combines the convenience of the new with the appearance of the old.

Generally speaking, the fittings you should go for are best based on Victorian or Edwardian designs. Aim for faded grandeur as modest designs are more in keeping with the country house. A high-level water cistern above the toilet may be authentic, but in a country cottage it is doubtful that you could fit one in because of the low ceilings in these buildings. Should it be possible, it may still appear too pompous in a room that is otherwise down-to-earth in its design.

Simple colours, natural materials

As the bathroom is a place to relax and cleanse yourself, a simple colour scheme is often the preferred choice. White or cream is a popular choice, as they give a fresh feel, and all other colours, as well as the colours of wood – from the yellow hues of pine through

below Reflected in the mirror you can see this dresser which boasts a marble top and dark green tiles which help inject a bit of colour into the bathroom.

to the dark tones of mahogany – are complemented by these clean shades. Other colours that also look good in the bathroom are blues and greens, because of their obvious connections to water, and soft pastel shades such as pink, lilac or lemon. These can look very pretty and are fun to play with in small cottage bathrooms, as their appearance makes a little room look really quite appealing.

There is no place more suited to pine panelling than the bathroom. Use it around the bath, to box in pipework, plumbing or the toilet cistern, and on the walls (either just on the lower half up to dado-rail height, or all the way up to the ceiling). Once it has been given a coat of varnish to make it waterproof, tongue and groove panelling is the perfect choice for the country bathroom interior. Wood looks fresh, clean and natural and is preferable to tiles, which look rather out of place in the country bathroom. A few tiles, particularly hand-painted rustic designs, judiciously used for a splashback against the basin, may be possible to get away with, but certainly tiling the whole room should be avoided as the results are far too modern and clinical. If yours is a busy family bathroom, a few rows of tiles around the bath may be in order, but otherwise they are best avoided when creating a country-style feel.

The beauty of pine panelling is that if an all-wood finish isn't to your taste, the panelling can be colourwashed to allow the grain of the wood to show through. Alternatively it can be limed to give it a pale white finish, stained with wood stain in a variety of colours or simply painted any colour you choose.

Most of the bathrooms shown here are striking in their simplicity. White walls are teamed with mahogany wood and

opposite The window dressings, opulent gold-framed mirror and large bouquet of flowers combine to give this bathroom a very stylish feminine appearance.

left Pine tongue and groove panelling is perfect for boxing in the bath. It can be left plain, or stained, varnished or painted to suit your colour scheme.

right Swags of fabrics, layered at the window to form a loosely draping pelmet, are simply wound around a metal curtain pole.

below *An all-white bathroom looks clean and refreshing and shows off the original beams to their best advantage. However, the look is prevented from appearing too clinical by the addition of plenty of accessories.*

mirror panels, a room is simply painted candy pink, or white panelling is teamed with a quaint miniature print wallpaper.

Furniture and accessories

Marine styling is always at home in the country bathroom. Obvious ways in which a seaside style can be introduced are with a blue-and-white colour scheme, or via a display of accessories such as pebbles, or other beach paraphernalia. Painting bath panelling white also imparts a marine feel and because the seaside is part of nature, it is a theme that works well in a country-style bathroom. To continue the theme, accessories such as mirrors or bath racks made from driftwood, or fabrics and wallpapers with shell, shipping or fish motifs should be chosen.

Window treatments can vary from having nothing at all at the windows (providing you are not overlooked), to simple floral cotton curtains teamed with a pelmet in a contrasting floral fabric, or ornate dressings of sheer fabrics such as muslin or voile, arranged to make an interesting, soft, rather romantic pelmet design.

Additional furniture and accessories are important in the country-style bathroom because what you are trying to create is a safe haven and a place for relaxation. So, unless space is really at a

left and below A little cupboard filled with perfumes and make-up makes a nice display and bowls and arrangements of shells are all very interesting. Even the pot of petunias is co-ordinated with the colour scheme.

premium the room can benefit from having an easy chair in the corner – perhaps an old Lloyd Loom or wicker chair painted white. If space is limited a little wrought-iron chair or a stool work well. A seat provides somewhere to relax while young children bathe, or at the very least a place to pile clothes instead of on the floor. Tables or shelves can be used to show off collections as well as provide storage for bathroom essentials such as mirrors, brushes and toiletries. Bath racks, whose use was common in Victorian times, are a welcome addition to the country bathroom, particularly if they are made of wood. A pine duck-board on the floor makes a suitable alternative to the bath mat, although a small rag rug is an authentic addition. Free-standing wooden clothes-horses were used in Victorian bathrooms and a contemporary pine version is perfect placed in front of the window. Modern-day necessities such as shower curtains are best made from cotton fabric and lined with plastic to make them waterproof, as the modern plastic versions have no place in a country-style setting. An alternative decorative idea is to use a Victorian screen, which would have been used to change behind in the bedroom, as a screen for bathing behind.

Don't forget to inject a bit of life and nature into the bathroom with well-chosen flowers and plants. Many plants enjoy the moist, damp atmosphere of the bathroom and a bunch of flowers can make all the difference. You'll notice how all the bathrooms featured here contain either plants or flowers, which is very much part of their appeal.

opposite Even the beams have been painted white in this all-white bathroom. A few oriental accessories, dotted here and there, make the room more interesting.

left This tiny window needs no dressings as it looks out over roof tops. A pot plant is all that's required by way of decoration.

right Old-fashioned pillar taps suit the basin in this bathroom, and the tiny Shaker-inspired peg rail on the wall is the perfect place for hand towels.

PICTURE CREDITS

The author and publishers are grateful to Elizabeth Whiting Associates and to the following photographers for their kind permission to reproduce the photographs on the following pages: 2, 11, 13, 30, 32–3, 36–8, 46, 58–9, 85–7, 90–3 Lu Jeffrey; 6, 14–15, 29, 77, 84 Spike Powell; 8, 63, 68, 72–3, 81 Di Lewis; 9 16–17, 22, 40–1, 64–5 Michael Dunne; 18, 50–51 Mark Luscombe-Whyte; 20–21, 31, 34–5, 82–3, 88–9 Dennis Stone; 24–5 Tim Beddow; 27, 31, 48–9 Nick Carter; 42–3, 86 Andreas v. Einsiedel; 45, 54–6, 66–7 Brian Harrison; 52–3, 61, 78–9 Simon Upton; 70–1 EWA; 74–5 Huntley Hedworth; 76 Nadia MacKenzie; 94–5 Bruce Hemmings.